50 Gourmet Dinner for Two Recipes

By: Kelly Johnson

Table of Contents

- Filet Mignon with Red Wine Sauce
- Lobster Tail with Garlic Butter
- Pan-Seared Duck Breast with Cherry Sauce
- Beef Wellington
- Seared Scallops with Lemon Herb Butter
- Grilled Salmon with Dill Cream Sauce
- Chicken Marsala
- Shrimp Scampi with Linguine
- Braised Short Ribs with Mashed Potatoes
- Roasted Rack of Lamb with Rosemary
- Pan-Seared Veal Chops with Truffle Oil
- Stuffed Chicken Breast with Spinach and Goat Cheese
- Grilled Tuna Steaks with Sesame Crust
- Crab Cakes with Remoulade Sauce
- Lobster Ravioli in Creamy Alfredo Sauce
- Risotto with Asparagus and Parmesan
- Grilled Filet of Beef with Béarnaise Sauce
- Blackened Halibut with Mango Salsa
- Herb-Crusted Salmon with Pesto
- Duck Confit with Potato Gratin
- Grilled Ribeye Steak with Chimichurri Sauce
- Eggplant Parmesan
- Seared Ahi Tuna with Wasabi Sauce
- Roasted Beet and Goat Cheese Salad
- Chicken Cacciatore
- Veal Scallopini with Lemon Butter Sauce
- Lobster Newberg
- Braised Chicken Thighs with Olives and Lemon
- Seared Cod with Tomato Basil Sauce
- Pappardelle with Wild Mushroom Sauce
- Pork Tenderloin with Apple Cider Reduction
- Sea Bass with Caper and Lemon Butter Sauce
- Pan-Seared Duck Breast with Orange Glaze
- Baked Ziti with Sausage and Ricotta
- Grilled Shrimp with Garlic and Lime

- Stuffed Bell Peppers with Quinoa and Feta
- Peking Duck with Hoisin Sauce
- Veal Milanese with Arugula Salad
- Grilled Vegetable Medley with Balsamic Glaze
- Lobster Mac and Cheese
- Grilled Swordfish with Tomato Basil Relish
- Seared Pork Belly with Apple Slaw
- Beef and Mushroom Stroganoff
- Grilled Lamb Chops with Mint Yogurt Sauce
- Chicken Piccata with Lemon and Capers
- Smoked Salmon with Cucumber Dill Salad
- Baked Sea Trout with Lemon and Thyme
- Stuffed Portobello Mushrooms with Parmesan
- Salmon en Papillote with Vegetables
- Wild Mushroom and Truffle Oil Risotto

Filet Mignon with Red Wine Sauce

Ingredients:

- 2 filet mignon steaks (6 oz each)
- Salt and pepper to taste
- 2 tbsp olive oil
- 2 tbsp unsalted butter
- 1/2 cup red wine (preferably dry)
- 1/4 cup beef broth
- 2 cloves garlic, minced
- 1 shallot, finely chopped
- 1 sprig fresh thyme

Instructions:

1. Preheat the oven to 400°F (200°C).
2. Season the filet mignon steaks with salt and pepper.
3. In an ovenproof skillet, heat the olive oil over medium-high heat.
4. Sear the steaks for 3-4 minutes on each side until browned.
5. Transfer the skillet to the oven and roast for 5-7 minutes, or until desired doneness.
6. Remove the steaks from the skillet and set aside to rest.
7. In the same skillet, melt the butter over medium heat. Add the garlic, shallot, and thyme, and sauté for 1-2 minutes.
8. Pour in the red wine and beef broth, scraping the brown bits from the bottom of the pan.
9. Simmer for 5-7 minutes until the sauce reduces by half.
10. Serve the steaks with the red wine sauce drizzled on top.

Lobster Tail with Garlic Butter
Ingredients:

- 4 lobster tails
- 1/2 cup unsalted butter, melted
- 3 cloves garlic, minced
- 1 tbsp lemon juice
- 1 tbsp chopped fresh parsley
- Salt and pepper to taste

Instructions:

1. Preheat the oven to 375°F (190°C).
2. Use kitchen shears to cut along the top of the lobster tails, exposing the meat.
3. Gently lift the meat out of the shell and lay it on top, leaving the tail shell intact.
4. In a small bowl, combine the melted butter, garlic, lemon juice, and parsley.
5. Brush the lobster meat with the garlic butter mixture and season with salt and pepper.
6. Place the lobster tails on a baking sheet and bake for 12-15 minutes, or until the meat is opaque and tender.
7. Serve with additional garlic butter for dipping.

Pan-Seared Duck Breast with Cherry Sauce
Ingredients:

- 2 duck breasts
- Salt and pepper to taste
- 1 tbsp olive oil
- 1/2 cup red wine
- 1/2 cup chicken broth
- 1/4 cup cherry preserves
- 2 tbsp balsamic vinegar
- 1 tbsp butter

Instructions:

1. Preheat the oven to 400°F (200°C).
2. Score the skin of the duck breasts in a crisscross pattern and season with salt and pepper.
3. Heat the olive oil in a skillet over medium-high heat.
4. Place the duck breasts skin-side down and sear for 5-7 minutes, until the skin is crispy.
5. Flip the duck breasts and sear for an additional 2-3 minutes.
6. Transfer the skillet to the oven and roast for 6-8 minutes, or until the duck reaches your desired doneness.
7. Remove the duck from the skillet and let it rest.
8. In the same skillet, add the red wine, chicken broth, cherry preserves, and balsamic vinegar.
9. Bring to a simmer and cook for 5-7 minutes, until the sauce thickens.
10. Stir in the butter and season with salt and pepper.
11. Slice the duck breasts and serve with the cherry sauce.

Beef Wellington
Ingredients:

- 2 lb beef tenderloin, trimmed
- Salt and pepper to taste
- 2 tbsp olive oil
- 8 oz cremini mushrooms, finely chopped
- 2 tbsp unsalted butter
- 1/4 cup dry white wine
- 2 tbsp Dijon mustard
- 1 sheet puff pastry
- 1 egg, beaten

Instructions:

1. Preheat the oven to 400°F (200°C).
2. Season the beef tenderloin with salt and pepper.
3. Heat olive oil in a skillet over medium-high heat. Sear the beef on all sides for 2-3 minutes.
4. Remove the beef from the skillet and brush with Dijon mustard. Let cool.
5. In the same skillet, melt the butter and sauté the mushrooms for 5-7 minutes until browned. Add the white wine and cook for another 2 minutes.
6. Let the mushroom mixture cool, then spread it evenly over the beef.
7. Roll out the puff pastry and place the beef in the center. Fold the pastry over the beef and seal the edges.
8. Brush the pastry with the beaten egg.
9. Bake for 30-35 minutes, or until the pastry is golden and the beef reaches your desired doneness.
10. Let rest before slicing and serving.

Seared Scallops with Lemon Herb Butter
Ingredients:

- 12 large sea scallops
- Salt and pepper to taste
- 2 tbsp olive oil
- 3 tbsp unsalted butter
- 2 cloves garlic, minced
- 1 tbsp fresh lemon juice
- 1 tbsp chopped fresh parsley

Instructions:

1. Pat the scallops dry with paper towels and season with salt and pepper.
2. Heat the olive oil in a skillet over medium-high heat.
3. Add the scallops and sear for 2-3 minutes on each side until golden brown and opaque.
4. Remove the scallops from the skillet and set aside.
5. In the same skillet, melt the butter and sauté the garlic for 1 minute.
6. Stir in the lemon juice and parsley.
7. Return the scallops to the skillet and toss to coat with the lemon herb butter.
8. Serve immediately.

Grilled Salmon with Dill Cream Sauce

Ingredients:

- 4 salmon fillets
- Salt and pepper to taste
- 2 tbsp olive oil
- 1/2 cup sour cream
- 2 tbsp mayonnaise
- 1 tbsp fresh dill, chopped
- 1 tbsp lemon juice

Instructions:

1. Preheat the grill to medium-high heat.
2. Season the salmon fillets with salt and pepper and brush with olive oil.
3. Grill the salmon for 4-5 minutes per side, or until cooked through.
4. In a small bowl, combine the sour cream, mayonnaise, dill, and lemon juice.
5. Serve the grilled salmon with the dill cream sauce on top.

Chicken Marsala
Ingredients:

- 4 boneless, skinless chicken breasts
- Salt and pepper to taste
- 1/4 cup flour
- 2 tbsp olive oil
- 1/2 cup Marsala wine
- 1/2 cup chicken broth
- 1/2 cup heavy cream
- 1/4 cup fresh parsley, chopped

Instructions:

1. Season the chicken breasts with salt and pepper, then dredge them in flour.
2. Heat the olive oil in a skillet over medium-high heat.
3. Cook the chicken breasts for 4-5 minutes per side until golden brown and cooked through.
4. Remove the chicken from the skillet and set aside.
5. Add the Marsala wine to the skillet and scrape up any brown bits.
6. Stir in the chicken broth and heavy cream and simmer for 5 minutes.
7. Return the chicken to the skillet and simmer for an additional 5 minutes.
8. Garnish with fresh parsley and serve.

Shrimp Scampi with Linguine
Ingredients:

- 12 oz linguine
- 1 lb large shrimp, peeled and deveined
- Salt and pepper to taste
- 2 tbsp olive oil
- 3 tbsp unsalted butter
- 4 cloves garlic, minced
- 1/4 tsp red pepper flakes
- 1/4 cup dry white wine
- 1/4 cup fresh lemon juice
- 1 tbsp fresh parsley, chopped

Instructions:

1. Cook the linguine according to package directions and drain.
2. Season the shrimp with salt and pepper.
3. Heat the olive oil and butter in a skillet over medium-high heat.
4. Add the shrimp and cook for 2-3 minutes per side until pink.
5. Remove the shrimp from the skillet and set aside.
6. In the same skillet, sauté the garlic and red pepper flakes for 1 minute.
7. Add the white wine and lemon juice and simmer for 2 minutes.
8. Return the shrimp to the skillet and toss with the linguine.
9. Garnish with fresh parsley and serve immediately.

Braised Short Ribs with Mashed Potatoes
Ingredients:

- 4 bone-in short ribs
- Salt and pepper to taste
- 2 tbsp olive oil
- 1 onion, chopped
- 2 carrots, chopped
- 2 celery stalks, chopped
- 4 cloves garlic, minced
- 1 cup red wine
- 3 cups beef broth
- 1 tbsp tomato paste
- 2 sprigs fresh thyme
- 2 bay leaves
- 4 cups mashed potatoes (prepared)

Instructions:

1. Preheat the oven to 325°F (165°C).
2. Season the short ribs with salt and pepper.
3. Heat olive oil in a large Dutch oven over medium-high heat.
4. Sear the short ribs on all sides until browned, about 8 minutes.
5. Remove the short ribs and set aside. In the same pot, add the onion, carrots, celery, and garlic. Sauté for 5 minutes until softened.
6. Add the red wine, scraping up any brown bits from the bottom of the pot. Stir in the tomato paste, beef broth, thyme, and bay leaves.
7. Return the short ribs to the pot, cover, and transfer to the oven. Braise for 2-3 hours, until the ribs are tender.
8. Serve the short ribs over mashed potatoes and drizzle with the braising liquid.

Roasted Rack of Lamb with Rosemary

Ingredients:

- 1 rack of lamb (8 ribs)
- Salt and pepper to taste
- 2 tbsp olive oil
- 2 cloves garlic, minced
- 2 tbsp fresh rosemary, chopped
- 1 tbsp Dijon mustard
- 1 tbsp balsamic vinegar

Instructions:

1. Preheat the oven to 400°F (200°C).
2. Season the rack of lamb with salt and pepper.
3. Heat olive oil in a skillet over medium-high heat. Sear the lamb on all sides for 3-4 minutes until browned.
4. In a small bowl, combine garlic, rosemary, Dijon mustard, and balsamic vinegar. Rub the mixture over the lamb.
5. Place the lamb in the oven and roast for 15-20 minutes for medium-rare, or longer for desired doneness.
6. Let rest for 5 minutes before slicing and serving.

Pan-Seared Veal Chops with Truffle Oil
Ingredients:

- 2 veal chops
- Salt and pepper to taste
- 2 tbsp olive oil
- 2 tbsp unsalted butter
- 2 cloves garlic, smashed
- 1 sprig fresh thyme
- 1 tbsp truffle oil

Instructions:

1. Season the veal chops with salt and pepper.
2. Heat olive oil in a skillet over medium-high heat. Add the veal chops and sear for 4-5 minutes on each side until golden brown.
3. Add the butter, garlic, and thyme to the skillet and cook for an additional 2-3 minutes, basting the veal with the melted butter.
4. Remove the veal chops from the skillet and drizzle with truffle oil.
5. Let rest for 5 minutes before serving.

Stuffed Chicken Breast with Spinach and Goat Cheese
Ingredients:

- 4 boneless, skinless chicken breasts
- Salt and pepper to taste
- 2 tbsp olive oil
- 1 cup fresh spinach, wilted
- 1/2 cup goat cheese, crumbled
- 2 tbsp sun-dried tomatoes, chopped
- 1/4 cup chicken broth

Instructions:

1. Preheat the oven to 375°F (190°C).
2. Season the chicken breasts with salt and pepper.
3. In a bowl, combine the wilted spinach, goat cheese, and sun-dried tomatoes.
4. Cut a pocket in each chicken breast and stuff with the spinach mixture.
5. Heat olive oil in a skillet over medium-high heat. Sear the chicken breasts for 4-5 minutes on each side until golden brown.
6. Transfer the chicken to the oven and bake for 15-20 minutes, or until fully cooked.
7. Remove the chicken and deglaze the skillet with chicken broth, scraping up any browned bits.
8. Serve the chicken with the pan sauce.

Grilled Tuna Steaks with Sesame Crust
Ingredients:

- 4 tuna steaks
- Salt and pepper to taste
- 2 tbsp olive oil
- 1/4 cup sesame seeds (white and black)
- 2 tbsp soy sauce
- 1 tbsp rice vinegar

Instructions:

1. Season the tuna steaks with salt and pepper.
2. Brush both sides with olive oil and press the sesame seeds onto the tuna steaks.
3. Preheat the grill to medium-high heat. Grill the tuna for 2-3 minutes per side, until the outside is golden but the inside remains rare.
4. In a small bowl, combine the soy sauce and rice vinegar. Drizzle over the tuna steaks before serving.

Crab Cakes with Remoulade Sauce
Ingredients:

- 1 lb lump crab meat
- 1/4 cup breadcrumbs
- 1/4 cup mayonnaise
- 1 egg, beaten
- 2 tbsp Dijon mustard
- 1 tbsp Worcestershire sauce
- 1/2 tsp Old Bay seasoning
- Salt and pepper to taste
- 2 tbsp olive oil (for frying)

For the Remoulade Sauce:

- 1/2 cup mayonnaise
- 1 tbsp Dijon mustard
- 1 tbsp lemon juice
- 1 tbsp capers, chopped
- 1 tbsp fresh parsley, chopped
- 1/2 tsp hot sauce

Instructions:

1. In a bowl, combine the crab meat, breadcrumbs, mayonnaise, egg, mustard, Worcestershire sauce, Old Bay, salt, and pepper. Mix gently to combine.
2. Form the mixture into patties.
3. Heat olive oil in a skillet over medium-high heat. Fry the crab cakes for 3-4 minutes per side, until golden brown.
4. For the remoulade sauce, whisk together mayonnaise, mustard, lemon juice, capers, parsley, and hot sauce.
5. Serve the crab cakes with the remoulade sauce.

Lobster Ravioli in Creamy Alfredo Sauce
Ingredients:

- 12 lobster ravioli (store-bought or homemade)
- 2 tbsp unsalted butter
- 1 cup heavy cream
- 1/2 cup grated Parmesan cheese
- 1/4 tsp garlic powder
- Salt and pepper to taste
- Fresh parsley, chopped (for garnish)

Instructions:

1. Cook the lobster ravioli according to package instructions.
2. In a skillet, melt the butter over medium heat. Add the heavy cream and simmer for 3-5 minutes.
3. Stir in the Parmesan cheese and garlic powder. Season with salt and pepper.
4. Toss the cooked ravioli in the creamy Alfredo sauce.
5. Garnish with fresh parsley and serve.

Risotto with Asparagus and Parmesan

Ingredients:

- 1 cup Arborio rice
- 1 tbsp olive oil
- 1 small onion, finely chopped
- 2 cloves garlic, minced
- 4 cups chicken broth (or vegetable broth)
- 1/2 cup white wine
- 1 bunch asparagus, trimmed and cut into 1-inch pieces
- 1/2 cup grated Parmesan cheese
- Salt and pepper to taste

Instructions:

1. In a large saucepan, heat the olive oil over medium heat.
2. Add the onion and garlic, and sauté for 3-4 minutes until softened.
3. Stir in the Arborio rice and cook for 1-2 minutes until lightly toasted.
4. Add the white wine and cook, stirring, until the liquid is absorbed.
5. Gradually add the chicken broth, one ladleful at a time, stirring constantly, until the rice is creamy and tender (about 18-20 minutes).
6. In the last 5 minutes of cooking, add the asparagus.
7. Stir in the Parmesan cheese and season with salt and pepper.
8. Serve immediately.

Grilled Filet of Beef with Béarnaise Sauce
Ingredients:

- 2 filet mignon steaks (6-8 oz each)
- Salt and pepper to taste
- 2 tbsp olive oil
- 1/2 cup white wine vinegar
- 2 tbsp shallots, minced
- 2 tbsp fresh tarragon, chopped
- 3 egg yolks
- 1/2 cup unsalted butter, melted
- 1 tbsp fresh lemon juice

Instructions:

1. Preheat the grill to high heat. Season the filet mignon steaks with salt and pepper.
2. Grill the steaks for about 4-5 minutes per side for medium-rare, or longer for desired doneness.
3. For the béarnaise sauce, in a small saucepan, combine the white wine vinegar, shallots, and half of the tarragon. Simmer for 2-3 minutes until reduced by half.
4. Strain the mixture into a bowl and whisk in the egg yolks.
5. Slowly add the melted butter, whisking constantly until the sauce thickens. Stir in the remaining tarragon and lemon juice.
6. Serve the grilled filet with the béarnaise sauce on top.

Blackened Halibut with Mango Salsa

Ingredients:

- 4 halibut fillets
- 2 tbsp blackening seasoning
- 2 tbsp olive oil
- 1 mango, diced
- 1/4 red onion, diced
- 1/4 cup cilantro, chopped
- 1 tbsp lime juice
- Salt and pepper to taste

Instructions:

1. Season the halibut fillets with blackening seasoning.
2. Heat olive oil in a skillet over medium-high heat. Cook the fillets for 3-4 minutes per side until golden and flaky.
3. In a bowl, combine the mango, red onion, cilantro, lime juice, salt, and pepper.
4. Serve the halibut fillets topped with the fresh mango salsa.

Herb-Crusted Salmon with Pesto
Ingredients:

- 4 salmon fillets
- 1/4 cup breadcrumbs
- 2 tbsp fresh parsley, chopped
- 1 tbsp fresh dill, chopped
- 1 tbsp fresh thyme, chopped
- 2 tbsp olive oil
- 1/4 cup pesto sauce (store-bought or homemade)

Instructions:

1. Preheat the oven to 400°F (200°C).
2. In a bowl, combine the breadcrumbs, parsley, dill, thyme, and a pinch of salt and pepper.
3. Brush the salmon fillets with olive oil and press the herb mixture onto the top of the fillets.
4. Place the salmon on a baking sheet and bake for 12-15 minutes, until the salmon is cooked through and the crust is golden.
5. Top each fillet with a spoonful of pesto sauce and serve.

Duck Confit with Potato Gratin

Ingredients:

- 4 duck legs
- Salt and pepper to taste
- 4 cloves garlic, smashed
- 2 sprigs fresh thyme
- 1 cup duck fat (or vegetable oil)
- 4 large potatoes, thinly sliced
- 1/2 cup heavy cream
- 1/2 cup milk
- 1 clove garlic, minced
- 1/2 cup grated Gruyère cheese

Instructions:

1. Preheat the oven to 300°F (150°C).
2. Season the duck legs with salt and pepper, then place them in a baking dish with garlic and thyme. Cover with duck fat and bake for 2-3 hours until tender.
3. For the potato gratin, layer the thinly sliced potatoes in a greased baking dish.
4. In a saucepan, heat the heavy cream, milk, and minced garlic over medium heat. Pour over the potatoes.
5. Sprinkle with grated Gruyère cheese and bake at 375°F (190°C) for 45 minutes until golden and bubbly.
6. Serve the duck confit alongside the creamy potato gratin.

Grilled Ribeye Steak with Chimichurri Sauce
Ingredients:

- 2 ribeye steaks
- Salt and pepper to taste
- 1/4 cup olive oil
- 2 tbsp red wine vinegar
- 1/4 cup fresh parsley, chopped
- 2 cloves garlic, minced
- 1/2 tsp red pepper flakes
- 1/2 tsp oregano

Instructions:

1. Preheat the grill to medium-high heat. Season the ribeye steaks with salt and pepper.
2. Grill the steaks for 4-5 minutes per side for medium-rare, or to your desired doneness.
3. For the chimichurri sauce, combine olive oil, red wine vinegar, parsley, garlic, red pepper flakes, oregano, salt, and pepper in a bowl.
4. Serve the grilled steaks topped with chimichurri sauce.

Eggplant Parmesan

Ingredients:

- 2 medium eggplants, sliced into 1/4-inch rounds
- Salt to taste
- 2 cups marinara sauce
- 2 cups mozzarella cheese, shredded
- 1/2 cup Parmesan cheese, grated
- 1/4 cup fresh basil, chopped
- 1/2 cup breadcrumbs
- 2 eggs, beaten
- Olive oil for frying

Instructions:

1. Salt the eggplant slices and let them sit for 30 minutes to draw out moisture. Pat dry with paper towels.
2. Preheat the oven to 375°F (190°C).
3. Dip the eggplant slices into beaten eggs and then coat in breadcrumbs.
4. Heat olive oil in a skillet and fry the eggplant slices until golden brown on both sides.
5. In a baking dish, layer fried eggplant slices with marinara sauce, mozzarella, and Parmesan. Repeat the layers.
6. Top with fresh basil and bake for 25-30 minutes until bubbly and golden.

Seared Ahi Tuna with Wasabi Sauce
Ingredients:

- 4 ahi tuna steaks
- Salt and pepper to taste
- 2 tbsp sesame seeds (optional)
- 1/4 cup soy sauce
- 1 tbsp rice vinegar
- 1 tbsp wasabi paste
- 1 tbsp honey

Instructions:

1. Season the tuna steaks with salt and pepper.
2. Optionally, coat the tuna with sesame seeds.
3. Heat a skillet over high heat and sear the tuna for 1-2 minutes per side for rare, or longer if desired.
4. In a small bowl, mix soy sauce, rice vinegar, wasabi paste, and honey.
5. Serve the seared tuna steaks with the wasabi sauce on the side.

Roasted Beet and Goat Cheese Salad

Ingredients:

- 4 medium beets, peeled and cut into wedges
- Olive oil for drizzling
- Salt and pepper to taste
- 4 cups mixed greens
- 1/2 cup goat cheese, crumbled
- 1/4 cup walnuts, toasted
- 2 tbsp balsamic glaze

Instructions:

1. Preheat the oven to 400°F (200°C).
2. Drizzle the beet wedges with olive oil, season with salt and pepper, and roast on a baking sheet for 25-30 minutes until tender.
3. In a large bowl, toss the mixed greens with roasted beets, goat cheese, and walnuts.
4. Drizzle with balsamic glaze and serve immediately.

Chicken Cacciatore

Ingredients:

- 4 bone-in, skin-on chicken thighs
- 2 tbsp olive oil
- Salt and pepper to taste
- 1 onion, chopped
- 2 cloves garlic, minced
- 1 bell pepper, sliced
- 1 can (14 oz) crushed tomatoes
- 1/2 cup red wine
- 1/4 cup kalamata olives, pitted and chopped
- 2 tbsp capers
- 1 tsp dried oregano
- 1/2 tsp red pepper flakes
- Fresh basil for garnish

Instructions:

1. Heat olive oil in a large skillet over medium-high heat. Season the chicken thighs with salt and pepper, then brown on both sides, about 5 minutes per side. Remove and set aside.
2. In the same skillet, sauté onion, garlic, and bell pepper until softened, about 5 minutes.
3. Add crushed tomatoes, red wine, olives, capers, oregano, and red pepper flakes. Stir well and bring to a simmer.
4. Return the chicken thighs to the skillet, skin-side up, and simmer for 30-40 minutes, until the chicken is cooked through.
5. Garnish with fresh basil and serve over pasta or with crusty bread.

Veal Scallopini with Lemon Butter Sauce

Ingredients:

- 4 veal cutlets
- Salt and pepper to taste
- 2 tbsp olive oil
- 2 tbsp butter
- 2 cloves garlic, minced
- 1/2 cup white wine
- 1/4 cup chicken broth
- Juice and zest of 1 lemon
- 2 tbsp fresh parsley, chopped

Instructions:

1. Season the veal cutlets with salt and pepper. Heat olive oil in a skillet over medium-high heat and cook the veal for 2-3 minutes per side until golden and cooked through. Remove and set aside.
2. In the same skillet, melt butter and sauté garlic for 1 minute.
3. Add white wine and chicken broth, scraping up any browned bits from the pan. Bring to a simmer and cook for 5 minutes.
4. Stir in lemon juice and zest, then return the veal to the pan, spooning the sauce over the meat.
5. Garnish with fresh parsley and serve.

Lobster Newberg

Ingredients:

- 2 lobster tails, cooked and chopped
- 4 egg yolks
- 1/2 cup heavy cream
- 1/4 cup brandy (or cognac)
- 1 tbsp butter
- 1/4 tsp cayenne pepper
- 1 tbsp lemon juice
- Salt and pepper to taste
- Fresh parsley for garnish

Instructions:

1. In a saucepan, melt butter over medium heat and sauté lobster meat for 2-3 minutes.
2. In a bowl, whisk together egg yolks, heavy cream, cayenne pepper, lemon juice, salt, and pepper.
3. Add the brandy to the pan with lobster meat and allow it to cook off, about 1 minute.
4. Slowly stir in the egg mixture, cooking gently over low heat until the sauce thickens.
5. Serve in a bowl or individual shells, garnished with fresh parsley.

Braised Chicken Thighs with Olives and Lemon

Ingredients:

- 4 bone-in, skin-on chicken thighs
- 2 tbsp olive oil
- Salt and pepper to taste
- 1 onion, chopped
- 2 cloves garlic, minced
- 1 cup white wine
- 1/2 cup chicken broth
- 1 cup green olives, pitted
- 1 lemon, thinly sliced
- Fresh thyme for garnish

Instructions:

1. Preheat oven to 375°F (190°C). Heat olive oil in a Dutch oven over medium-high heat. Season the chicken thighs with salt and pepper, then brown on both sides, about 4 minutes per side.
2. Remove chicken and set aside. In the same pot, sauté onion and garlic until softened, about 5 minutes.
3. Add white wine and chicken broth, scraping up any browned bits from the bottom of the pot.
4. Return chicken to the pot, adding olives, lemon slices, and thyme. Cover and transfer to the oven to braise for 40-45 minutes, until the chicken is tender.
5. Garnish with fresh thyme and serve with rice or mashed potatoes.

Seared Cod with Tomato Basil Sauce
Ingredients:

- 4 cod fillets
- Salt and pepper to taste
- 2 tbsp olive oil
- 1 can (14 oz) diced tomatoes
- 2 cloves garlic, minced
- 1/4 cup fresh basil, chopped
- 1 tsp sugar (optional)

Instructions:

1. Season cod fillets with salt and pepper. Heat olive oil in a skillet over medium-high heat and sear the cod for 3-4 minutes per side until golden and flaky. Remove from the pan and set aside.
2. In the same skillet, sauté garlic for 1 minute. Add diced tomatoes, sugar (if using), and a pinch of salt. Simmer for 10 minutes until the sauce thickens.
3. Stir in fresh basil and return the cod to the pan, spooning sauce over the fish.
4. Serve with steamed vegetables or pasta.

Pappardelle with Wild Mushroom Sauce
Ingredients:

- 1 lb pappardelle pasta
- 2 tbsp olive oil
- 2 cups wild mushrooms (such as chanterelles or cremini), sliced
- 1 shallot, minced
- 2 cloves garlic, minced
- 1/2 cup heavy cream
- 1/2 cup vegetable broth
- 1/4 cup fresh parsley, chopped
- Salt and pepper to taste

Instructions:

1. Cook the pappardelle according to package instructions. Drain and set aside.
2. Heat olive oil in a skillet over medium-high heat. Sauté mushrooms, shallot, and garlic until softened, about 5 minutes.
3. Add vegetable broth and bring to a simmer. Stir in heavy cream and cook until the sauce thickens, about 5 minutes.
4. Toss the cooked pasta with the mushroom sauce and garnish with fresh parsley.
5. Serve immediately.

Pork Tenderloin with Apple Cider Reduction

Ingredients:

- 1 pork tenderloin (about 1 lb)
- Salt and pepper to taste
- 2 tbsp olive oil
- 1/2 cup apple cider
- 1/4 cup chicken broth
- 2 tbsp Dijon mustard
- 1 tbsp fresh rosemary, chopped

Instructions:

1. Preheat the oven to 400°F (200°C). Season the pork tenderloin with salt and pepper.
2. Heat olive oil in an ovenproof skillet over medium-high heat. Brown the pork on all sides, about 5 minutes.
3. Transfer the skillet to the oven and roast for 20-25 minutes, until the pork reaches an internal temperature of 145°F (63°C).
4. Remove the pork and set aside. Add apple cider and chicken broth to the skillet, scraping up any browned bits.
5. Stir in Dijon mustard and rosemary, and cook until the sauce thickens, about 5 minutes.
6. Serve the pork sliced with the apple cider reduction sauce.

Sea Bass with Caper and Lemon Butter Sauce

Ingredients:

- 4 sea bass fillets
- Salt and pepper to taste
- 2 tbsp olive oil
- 2 tbsp butter
- 2 tbsp capers
- Juice of 1 lemon
- 1/4 cup fresh parsley, chopped

Instructions:

1. Season the sea bass fillets with salt and pepper.
2. Heat olive oil in a skillet over medium-high heat. Cook the fish for 3-4 minutes per side until golden and cooked through.
3. In the same skillet, melt butter and add capers and lemon juice. Cook for 1 minute, stirring to combine.
4. Pour the caper and lemon butter sauce over the cooked sea bass fillets.
5. Garnish with fresh parsley and serve with roasted vegetables or rice.

Pan-Seared Duck Breast with Orange Glaze

Ingredients:

- 2 duck breasts, skin on
- Salt and pepper to taste
- 1/2 cup fresh orange juice
- 2 tbsp honey
- 1 tbsp soy sauce
- 1 tsp cornstarch mixed with 1 tbsp water (optional for thickening)

Instructions:

1. Score the skin of the duck breasts in a criss-cross pattern. Season with salt and pepper.
2. Heat a skillet over medium-high heat. Place the duck breasts skin-side down and cook for about 6-8 minutes, until the skin is crispy and golden. Flip and cook for another 4-5 minutes, depending on your preferred doneness.
3. Remove the duck breasts and let them rest.
4. In the same skillet, add orange juice, honey, and soy sauce, scraping up any bits from the pan. Bring to a simmer and cook for 5 minutes.
5. If desired, add the cornstarch mixture to thicken the glaze.
6. Slice the duck breasts and drizzle with the orange glaze. Serve with roasted vegetables or mashed potatoes.

Baked Ziti with Sausage and Ricotta
Ingredients:

- 1 lb ziti pasta
- 1 lb Italian sausage, crumbled
- 1 jar (24 oz) marinara sauce
- 1 1/2 cups ricotta cheese
- 2 cups shredded mozzarella cheese
- 1/4 cup grated Parmesan cheese
- 1 tsp dried oregano
- Fresh basil for garnish

Instructions:

1. Preheat oven to 375°F (190°C).
2. Cook the ziti pasta according to package instructions, then drain.
3. In a skillet, cook the sausage over medium heat until browned. Add marinara sauce and oregano, and simmer for 10 minutes.
4. In a large bowl, combine cooked ziti, sausage sauce, ricotta, and half of the mozzarella cheese.
5. Transfer to a baking dish and top with remaining mozzarella and Parmesan cheese.
6. Bake for 20-25 minutes, until the cheese is melted and bubbly.
7. Garnish with fresh basil and serve.

Grilled Shrimp with Garlic and Lime

Ingredients:

- 1 lb large shrimp, peeled and deveined
- 2 tbsp olive oil
- 3 cloves garlic, minced
- Juice and zest of 1 lime
- 1/4 tsp red pepper flakes
- Salt and pepper to taste
- Fresh cilantro for garnish

Instructions:

1. In a bowl, combine olive oil, garlic, lime juice, lime zest, red pepper flakes, salt, and pepper. Add the shrimp and toss to coat. Marinate for 20 minutes.
2. Preheat the grill to medium-high heat.
3. Thread the shrimp onto skewers and grill for 2-3 minutes per side, until pink and cooked through.
4. Garnish with fresh cilantro and serve with rice or grilled vegetables.

Stuffed Bell Peppers with Quinoa and Feta

Ingredients:

- 4 bell peppers, tops cut off and seeds removed
- 1 cup quinoa, cooked
- 1 cup crumbled feta cheese
- 1 can (14 oz) diced tomatoes, drained
- 1/2 cup black olives, chopped
- 1 tsp dried oregano
- Salt and pepper to taste
- Fresh parsley for garnish

Instructions:

1. Preheat oven to 375°F (190°C).
2. In a large bowl, combine cooked quinoa, feta cheese, diced tomatoes, olives, oregano, salt, and pepper.
3. Stuff the bell peppers with the quinoa mixture and place in a baking dish.
4. Cover with foil and bake for 30 minutes, until the peppers are tender.
5. Garnish with fresh parsley and serve.

Peking Duck with Hoisin Sauce
Ingredients:

- 1 whole duck (about 5 lbs)
- 1 tbsp Chinese five-spice powder
- Salt to taste
- 2 tbsp honey
- 1/4 cup hoisin sauce
- 2 tbsp soy sauce
- 1 tbsp rice vinegar
- 1 cucumber, julienned
- 4-6 Chinese pancakes or soft flour tortillas

Instructions:

1. Preheat oven to 375°F (190°C).
2. Rub the duck inside and out with Chinese five-spice powder and salt.
3. Place the duck on a rack in a roasting pan and roast for 1 1/2 to 2 hours, until the skin is crispy and the duck is cooked through.
4. In a small saucepan, combine honey, hoisin sauce, soy sauce, and rice vinegar. Simmer for 5 minutes until thickened.
5. Slice the duck and serve with pancakes, hoisin sauce, cucumber, and optional scallions.

Veal Milanese with Arugula Salad

Ingredients:

- 4 veal cutlets
- Salt and pepper to taste
- 1 cup all-purpose flour
- 2 eggs, beaten
- 1 cup breadcrumbs
- 1/4 cup grated Parmesan cheese
- 3 tbsp olive oil
- 4 cups arugula
- 1/2 cup cherry tomatoes, halved
- Juice of 1 lemon

Instructions:

1. Season the veal cutlets with salt and pepper.
2. Dredge each cutlet in flour, dip in beaten eggs, and coat with breadcrumbs mixed with Parmesan cheese.
3. Heat olive oil in a skillet over medium-high heat. Cook the veal cutlets for 2-3 minutes per side until golden and crispy.
4. In a bowl, toss arugula and cherry tomatoes with lemon juice and a pinch of salt.
5. Serve the veal Milanese with the arugula salad on top.

Grilled Vegetable Medley with Balsamic Glaze

Ingredients:

- 1 zucchini, sliced
- 1 yellow squash, sliced
- 1 red bell pepper, sliced
- 1 red onion, sliced
- 2 tbsp olive oil
- Salt and pepper to taste
- 1/4 cup balsamic vinegar
- 1 tbsp honey

Instructions:

1. Preheat grill to medium-high heat.
2. Toss the vegetables in olive oil, salt, and pepper. Grill for 4-5 minutes per side until tender and lightly charred.
3. In a small saucepan, combine balsamic vinegar and honey. Bring to a simmer and cook for 5 minutes until thickened.
4. Drizzle the balsamic glaze over the grilled vegetables and serve warm.

Lobster Mac and Cheese
Ingredients:

- 1 lb elbow macaroni
- 2 tbsp butter
- 2 tbsp all-purpose flour
- 2 cups whole milk
- 2 cups shredded cheddar cheese
- 1/2 cup grated Parmesan cheese
- 1/2 tsp paprika
- 1/2 tsp garlic powder
- 1/4 tsp cayenne pepper
- 1/2 lb cooked lobster meat, chopped
- 1/2 cup panko breadcrumbs

Instructions:

1. Cook the macaroni according to package instructions and set aside.
2. In a saucepan, melt butter over medium heat. Stir in flour and cook for 1-2 minutes. Gradually whisk in milk and cook until the sauce thickens.
3. Stir in cheddar cheese, Parmesan cheese, paprika, garlic powder, and cayenne pepper.
4. Fold in the cooked lobster meat and macaroni.
5. Transfer to a baking dish and top with panko breadcrumbs. Bake at 375°F (190°C) for 15-20 minutes until golden and bubbly.
6. Serve hot.

Grilled Swordfish with Tomato Basil Relish

Ingredients:

- 4 swordfish steaks
- 2 tbsp olive oil
- Salt and pepper to taste
- 1 cup cherry tomatoes, halved
- 1/4 cup fresh basil, chopped
- 1 tbsp balsamic vinegar
- 1 tsp honey
- 1 clove garlic, minced
- 1 tbsp olive oil

Instructions:

1. Preheat grill to medium-high heat.
2. Brush swordfish steaks with olive oil and season with salt and pepper. Grill for 4-5 minutes per side until fish is cooked through and has grill marks.
3. In a bowl, combine cherry tomatoes, basil, balsamic vinegar, honey, garlic, and olive oil. Season with salt and pepper.
4. Serve swordfish topped with tomato basil relish.

Seared Pork Belly with Apple Slaw
Ingredients:

- 1 lb pork belly, cut into 1-inch strips
- Salt and pepper to taste
- 1 tbsp olive oil
- 2 cups shredded cabbage
- 1 apple, julienned
- 1/4 cup mayonnaise
- 1 tbsp apple cider vinegar
- 1 tsp Dijon mustard
- 1 tbsp honey
- 1/4 tsp celery seeds

Instructions:

1. Season pork belly strips with salt and pepper.
2. Heat olive oil in a skillet over medium-high heat. Sear pork belly strips for 4-5 minutes per side until crispy and cooked through.
3. In a bowl, combine cabbage, apple, mayonnaise, apple cider vinegar, Dijon mustard, honey, and celery seeds. Toss to combine.
4. Serve pork belly on a bed of apple slaw.

Beef and Mushroom Stroganoff
Ingredients:

- 1 lb beef sirloin, thinly sliced
- 1 tbsp olive oil
- 1 onion, finely chopped
- 2 cups mushrooms, sliced
- 2 cloves garlic, minced
- 1 cup beef broth
- 1/2 cup sour cream
- 1 tbsp Dijon mustard
- Salt and pepper to taste
- 2 tbsp fresh parsley, chopped
- Egg noodles for serving

Instructions:

1. Cook egg noodles according to package instructions. Set aside.
2. Heat olive oil in a large skillet over medium-high heat. Cook beef for 2-3 minutes until browned, then remove and set aside.
3. In the same skillet, sauté onion and mushrooms until softened, about 5 minutes. Add garlic and cook for another minute.
4. Stir in beef broth, sour cream, Dijon mustard, salt, and pepper. Return beef to the skillet and simmer for 5 minutes until the sauce thickens.
5. Serve beef stroganoff over egg noodles and garnish with parsley.

Grilled Lamb Chops with Mint Yogurt Sauce
Ingredients:

- 8 lamb chops
- 2 tbsp olive oil
- 2 tbsp fresh rosemary, chopped
- 2 cloves garlic, minced
- Salt and pepper to taste
- 1/2 cup Greek yogurt
- 2 tbsp fresh mint, chopped
- 1 tbsp lemon juice
- 1 tbsp honey

Instructions:

1. Preheat grill to medium-high heat.
2. Rub lamb chops with olive oil, rosemary, garlic, salt, and pepper. Grill for 4-5 minutes per side until desired doneness.
3. In a small bowl, combine Greek yogurt, mint, lemon juice, and honey. Season with salt and pepper.
4. Serve lamb chops with a side of mint yogurt sauce.

Chicken Piccata with Lemon and Capers
Ingredients:

- 4 boneless, skinless chicken breasts
- Salt and pepper to taste
- 1/2 cup flour
- 3 tbsp olive oil
- 1/4 cup fresh lemon juice
- 1/2 cup chicken broth
- 2 tbsp capers
- 2 tbsp fresh parsley, chopped

Instructions:

1. Season chicken breasts with salt and pepper, then dredge in flour.
2. Heat olive oil in a skillet over medium-high heat. Cook chicken for 4-5 minutes per side until golden and cooked through. Remove and set aside.
3. In the same skillet, add lemon juice, chicken broth, and capers. Bring to a simmer, scraping up any browned bits from the pan.
4. Return chicken to the skillet and cook for 2-3 minutes.
5. Serve with a sprinkle of fresh parsley.

Smoked Salmon with Cucumber Dill Salad
Ingredients:

- 8 oz smoked salmon, thinly sliced
- 1 cucumber, thinly sliced
- 1/4 cup red onion, thinly sliced
- 2 tbsp fresh dill, chopped
- 1 tbsp lemon juice
- 1 tbsp olive oil
- Salt and pepper to taste

Instructions:

1. Arrange smoked salmon slices on a platter.
2. In a bowl, combine cucumber, red onion, dill, lemon juice, and olive oil. Season with salt and pepper.
3. Spoon the cucumber dill salad over the smoked salmon. Serve immediately.

Baked Sea Trout with Lemon and Thyme
Ingredients:

- 2 sea trout fillets
- 1 lemon, sliced
- 2 sprigs fresh thyme
- 2 tbsp olive oil
- Salt and pepper to taste

Instructions:

1. Preheat oven to 375°F (190°C).
2. Place sea trout fillets on a baking sheet lined with parchment paper. Drizzle with olive oil and season with salt and pepper.
3. Top with lemon slices and thyme sprigs.
4. Bake for 15-20 minutes, or until fish is cooked through and flakes easily with a fork. Serve immediately.

Stuffed Portobello Mushrooms with Parmesan

Ingredients:

- 4 large portobello mushrooms, stems removed
- 1/2 cup breadcrumbs
- 1/4 cup grated Parmesan cheese
- 2 tbsp fresh parsley, chopped
- 2 tbsp olive oil
- 2 cloves garlic, minced
- Salt and pepper to taste

Instructions:

1. Preheat oven to 375°F (190°C).
2. Place portobello mushrooms on a baking sheet, gill side up.
3. In a bowl, combine breadcrumbs, Parmesan, parsley, garlic, olive oil, salt, and pepper.
4. Stuff the mushrooms with the breadcrumb mixture.
5. Bake for 20-25 minutes, until the mushrooms are tender and the topping is golden. Serve hot.

Salmon en Papillote with Vegetables
Ingredients:

- 2 salmon fillets
- 1 zucchini, thinly sliced
- 1 carrot, julienned
- 1/2 onion, thinly sliced
- 2 tbsp olive oil
- 1 lemon, sliced
- 2 sprigs fresh dill
- Salt and pepper to taste

Instructions:

1. Preheat oven to 400°F (200°C).
2. Cut two pieces of parchment paper large enough to fold over the salmon fillets.
3. Place the salmon fillets in the center of each piece of parchment.
4. Top with zucchini, carrot, onion, lemon slices, and dill. Drizzle with olive oil and season with salt and pepper.
5. Fold the parchment over the fish and vegetables to create a sealed packet.
6. Bake for 15-20 minutes, until the salmon is cooked through. Serve immediately.

Wild Mushroom and Truffle Oil Risotto

Ingredients:

- 1 cup Arborio rice
- 2 tbsp olive oil
- 1/2 cup onion, finely chopped
- 2 cups wild mushrooms, sliced
- 1/2 cup dry white wine
- 4 cups chicken or vegetable broth, warmed
- 1/2 cup Parmesan cheese, grated
- 2 tbsp fresh parsley, chopped
- 2 tsp truffle oil
- Salt and pepper to taste

Instructions:

1. In a large pan, heat olive oil over medium heat. Add onion and cook for 2-3 minutes until softened.
2. Add mushrooms and cook for 5-7 minutes until tender.
3. Stir in Arborio rice and cook for 1-2 minutes until the rice is lightly toasted.
4. Add white wine and cook until absorbed.
5. Gradually add warm broth, one ladle at a time, stirring constantly. Wait until the liquid is absorbed before adding more broth. Continue until the rice is tender and creamy, about 20 minutes.
6. Stir in Parmesan cheese, parsley, and truffle oil. Season with salt and pepper. Serve immediately.

www.ingramcontent.com/pod-product-compliance
Lightning Source LLC
LaVergne TN
LVHW081338060526
838201LV00055B/2718